SHINE!

WHAT IT MEANS TO BE A BIBLICAL CHRISTIAN

ROB SISCO

A rewrite of the booklet "Are You A Christian" by Rob Sisco

All Scripture quotations are taken from the King James Version.

Special emphasis in verses is added.

Written and Published by: Rob Sisco 2022

Edited by: Meghan Ward

ISBN: 978-0-578-42874-1

DEDICATION

While several could be mentioned, this book is dedicated to those men and women who, in my life, have been a consistent demonstration of what it means to be a Christian.

In particular, I make mention of dedication to:

Pastor Bud Silva – As my father-in-law, I have been able to observe first hand, behind the curtains so-to-speak, a man who is the "real deal." His consistency and convictions are not for the pulpit only, but are exemplified in his everyday life.

Dr. Ken Adrian – The pastor of my youth, Ken Adrian was, in my view, the picture of hospitality, compassion, and love for others. He remains one of the godliest men I've ever known.

CONTENTS

Introduction...................................9

ONE- Christian Deception....................11

TWO- Are You A Christian?..................25

THREE- A New Birth..........................37

FOUR- Grow Up!...............................45

FIVE- Shine!....................................63

SIX- Be Peculiar!...............................73

SEVEN- Get Busy!..............................81

EIGHT- Sacrifice!...............................85

Final Thoughts................................93

INTRODUCTION

People often use terms such as "good" Christian or "bad" Christian to label neighbors, co-workers, or church members, but is there really such a thing? John R. Rice challenged a generation by reminding us that "you are the best Christian somebody knows." To that I agree and understand his heart to provoke others to holiness. However, are there really good or bad Christians?

The Bible indicates that there are not. There are only Christians or non-Christians. A biblical Christian is a Christ-follower and someone is either following Christ in their daily life or they are not. You and I can be saved, on our way to heaven, and not be a true Christ-follower.

For a few years I was actively involved in the rodeo. I was a bull rider. By the age of twenty-five I stopped riding bulls and regularly hanging around rodeos. Now that I do not ride anymore, I no longer tell people that I am a bull rider. I may tell someone that I used to ride, but to state that I am a bull rider would suggest that I'm still riding and be inaccurate for me to say.

The same is true for many Christians. They used to be Christ followers, but because of the lust of the flesh, lust of the eyes, and/or the pride of life, they have stopped following Christ. It would be far more accurate for this one to say "I used to be a Christian" than "I am a Christian."

At the age of nine years old, I trusted Christ as my personal Savior. Through stretches of my teenage years, and even further into my early adult years, I often times found myself walking in the flesh, living to fulfill the lusts of my own comfort and pleasure. I did not lose my salvation - the Bible clearly teaches that once a man is saved he is always saved - but I certainly was not following Christ.

While many may argue that this approach is nothing more than semantics, this book is written to present a biblical picture of a true Christian- to reaching those who need the Gospel and to stir up those who do know Christ to be the Christ-following disciples we are called to be.

It is not the author's intention to write another discipleship book. Many have done a great job of this already. Rather, it my desire to remind the reader of the general biblical characteristics of a true Christ-follower. It is my prayer that we would get back to biblical Christianity and shine!

CHAPTER ONE

CHRISTIAN DECEPTION

It has happened on more than one occasion. While visiting with someone I've just met, I explain;

"I am the pastor of Valley Bible Baptist Church. We would love to have you visit with us this Sunday morning!"

With uncertainty and hesitation, the reply comes in some form of the question, "A Baptist church... but are you Christian?"

No matter how often I have been asked this question, it still amazes me. I have never been one to shy away from telling people that the churches I've pastored are Baptist churches. In fact, I want our guests to know. For those who do not know what a Baptist is, it really won't mean much, but for those who do know, I do not wish to hide it from them.

I find it remarkable that some would have no idea that Baptists are Christians.

"Are you a Christian?"

Emphatically, "Yes!"

A simple question that usually yields no real thought to answer. Yet this simple question is often misunderstood, confused, and deserves much deeper Scriptural understanding.

In the United States, approximately seventy-five percent of the population classify themselves as "Christian."[1] Evident in the increasing rise of the megachurch, the seeker-sensitive movement has proven the capable of amassing great crowds of people.

There has also been a great interest in our country in nondenominational movements such as Promise Keepers, World Council of Churches, and the Gospel Coalition which seek to tear down the walls of denominational differences and purportedly draw more people into Christianity.

In addition, the Christian music market is a rapidly growing business as more and more pop musicians, rock-n-roll artists, and rappers sing about Jesus.

Affiliation with these types of movements has led to a majority of Americans calling themselves Christian. While some classify themselves as Christians only because they are American, others stake a claim on Christianity because their parents raised them in church. Many more have established a relationship or membership in an organization that classifies as Christian, so they believe that makes them a Christian.

Nothing New

Throughout the last two thousand years, the generalization and hijacking of the name given to God's people has been present. It is really nothing new. This is undoubtedly displeasing to the Lord, as well as misleading to the cause of Christ.

The name Christian has been improperly used to categorize many false teachers and even villains of the Gospel. Peter warns of this:

*"But there were false prophets also among the people, even as there shall be **false teachers among you**, who privily shall bring in damnable heresies, even denying the Lord that bought them, and bring upon themselves swift destruction. And many shall follow there pernicious ways…"*

– II Peter 2:1,2

These false prophets and teachers existed during the time of the patriarchs, apostles, and throughout church history. Peter used the word "privily" to describe how they would come. They do not bring attention to themselves by looking and acting like false teachers; they do it privately or discretely. Jude makes a similar statement when dealing with apostasy:

"For there were certain men crept in unawares…"

– Jude 4

Jesus describes the false teacher as a "wolf in sheep's clothing." Masquerading themselves in the form of a Christian, they identify themselves as such. In spite of their lure and ability to blend in with others, they will lead people into "pernicious," or destructive ways.

One of Satan's greatest tools to use against people is deception. This is evident in the ever-increasing interest of the U.F.O. phenomena, as well as a growing desire to know and understand the paranormal. To any true Bible believer, this is undeniably the work of the Devil. While some may indeed see incredible things, and even experience strange occurrences, it is apparent to the Bible student that the "Great Deceiver" is working very hard to take men's eyes off of the Bible.

Similarly, Satan uses false doctrine and false teaching to steer minds away from God's Word and mankind's need for a Savior. Far too many "Christians" and "churches" emphasize experiences and emotions above the written Word of God. One might say, "…Yes, but you don't know what I felt!" My reply to that is, "No, but I know what the Bible says and God will not make an exception for you when it is contrary to His Word."

Easily Deceived

No one wants to think of themselves as being deceived, yet Peter warned that many would follow false teaching as destructive doctrines permeated homes and churches.

To mention every false teaching out there would require a library of books, but in a simple effort to illustrate, we will briefly highlight two prevalent teachings found in "Christian" churches in every city.

Emphasized in Pentecostal churches, but increasingly infiltrating many others, the contemporary teaching of tongues is in shocking contrast to God's Word. The Apostle Paul said tongues are *"for a sign, not to them that believe, but to them that believe not."* Yet many "believers" are in awe over their experience. Furthermore, the Bible shows us that only men ever spoke in tongues, yet women are often the driving force of its current teaching.

Contrary to modern teaching, tongues in the Bible were natural human languages, unknown to either the hearer or speaker, which were understood under a miraculous giving of the Holy Spirit. The gift of tongues was always associated with souls coming to Christ and never for the purpose of a "Christian" having a divine, out-of-body experience. In 1 Corinthians 12-14, Paul makes it abundantly clear that tongues were not a learned trait or emphasized gift.

Our faith should not hinge upon a sign, but rather on the written and infallible Word of God.

"So then faith cometh by hearing, and hearing by the word of God."

- Romans 10:17

Another troubling teaching that has ravaged its way into "Christianity" is that of "radical grace." The idea of this teaching is, "I am saved by grace, and therefore have the liberty to do what I want." To this Paul states:

"What shall we say then? Shall we continue in sin, that grace may abound? **God forbid.** *How shall we, that are dead to sin, live any longer therein?"*

- Romans 6:1-2

The Bible's clear teaching on holiness in the life of a believer produces no effect on those that have been deceived by this destructive doctrine. How happy Satan must be when a child of God falls into this snare. He knows that by getting you to live against God's clear will for your life, you (in turn) will have no effect on others.

If you know Christ as your Savior, you were not saved so that you could live any way you please, rather you were saved to live for Christ. The motto of the Christian life should be "Nevertheless I live, yet not I, but Christ!"

Christian Religion?

Many false teachers, heretics, and villains have and will continue to use the name of Christ to hide private agendas and destructive motives. I presume that many of these never realize for whom they work and, in a sense, are not intentionally deceiving people. God, however, gives no discretion or exception to His infinite justice. He has given us the truth in His Word and those that diligently seek the truth shall find it.

I think of the many Mormon missionaries who travel from house to house presenting the Mormon "church" to be a family-orientated place. In reality, the deep, dark secrets of the Latter Day Saints (LDS) organization point to lives destroyed and families alienated and torn apart from one another simply because one member may disagree with LDS teaching.

The missionary, whether through naivety or negligence, goes from house to house praising an organization covering dark secrets. Unknowing or not, the deception continues and is without excuse.

Without a doubt, the most visual and the most influential religious group in "Christendom" is the Roman Catholic Church (RCC). To the ignorant eye, the Pope and hierarchy of the RCC are the epitome of Christianity. In spite of centuries of history that show the RCC persecuting true believers and with involvement in cover-ups and conspiracies, the RCC is considered a leader in the religious realm of Christianity throughout the world.

Much time could be spent discussing the many denominations, groups, churches, and movements, all of which classify themselves as Christian. The following list is only intended to list a few of these:

Denominations and Churches:

Apostolic	Assembly of God	Anglican
Baptist	Church of Christ	Episcopal
Lutheran	Church of God	Methodist
Pentecostal	Presbyterian	RCC

Movements, Groups, & Labels:

Charismatic	Gospel Coalition	Fundamental
Evangelical	Promise Keepers	WCC

There is only one Christ, and one doctrine that Christ taught. Many times as a pastor I have been asked, "Why are there so many different denominations?" The answer is quite simply: "men crept in unawares." Every group, denomination, and church listed above claims to have the truth, but every one of them differ from one another in their teaching.

Many men see this division as a reason to separate and begin non-denominational churches or movements. This idea does not remove false teaching, but rather integrates it as members from various belief systems move in. The solution is not to begin some new thing, but to get back to preaching the Word and nothing but the Word! The answer for the Christian is to "earnestly contend for the faith!"

I am a Baptist preacher. I am a Baptist by conviction and I will always be a Baptist. I emphatically believe that the Baptist people can trace a lineage of doctrine all the way back to Christ and the apostles. Being a Baptist, however, does not mean that I am always right. On the contrary, I am often wrong, but the Bible is always right and the Bible must be the source of all of my faith and practice!

However, that is not the heart of the "false teacher." That is not the heart even of the typical "Christian." Far too many could take or leave the clear teachings of Scripture: that is not Christianity.

Faces of Christianity

I am overwhelmed by what I see in America today as, I am sure, are most Bible-believing preachers. God must be displeased by what He sees, not only on the streets of our cities and towns, but also in the so-called "Christian" churches that are to be a beacon of light to the lost.

Sadly, today it is acceptable for a man to identify as a Christian even though his life proves otherwise. We find that open homosexuality, fornication, idolatry, disobedience and many other forms of wicked lifestyles are commonplace in churches and in "Christian" lives.

From spiritual leaders who have long ago abandoned principled lives, and privately harbor vile sin in their hearts, to church members who defend debauchery and abominable life practices that would cause the previous generation to blush in shame. Something is wrong!

As Christians, we wrongly identify many things with a Christian label that may or may not be so. For example, when we spot someone wearing a cross, we often say, "They must be a Christian." If a football player points to the sky after scoring a touchdown, we idolize him and state, "He must be a Christian." When a politician attends a prayer breakfast, to far too many it becomes equivalent to a sinner confessing their sin and therefore we say, "They must be a Christian."

Several years ago while driving through town, I saw a sticker on the back of a car window that stated "Jesus Loves You!" I admired the boldness of the person and immediately thought to myself, "They must be a Christian." The moment that thought came to my mind, I spotted the drivers hand come out of the window with a lit cigarette in it. I'll admit the driver may or may not be a born-again believer, but what kind of testimony is that?! What message is sent to the unbeliever who sees that same thing?

In 2nd Corinthians, Paul describes what God desires of us as Christians: a Christian is to practice separation from the world.

"Be ye not unequally yoked together with unbelievers: for what fellowship hath righteousness with unrighteousness? And what communion hath light with darkness?"

- 2 Corinthians 6:14

As a young boy scout, I recall going on a trip to some lava caves in northern Arizona. We entered a huge underground cave network that seemed to be a mile deep. Though many portions of the cave were very narrow, we eventually entered a portion that was a large, open area. While in this section, we all turned our flashlights off in order to see how dark it would be. With absolutely no light coming into the space, I could not even see my hand in front of my face. But the moment one boy turned his flashlight back on, all the darkness left the room. This is what Paul is describing here in 2nd Corinthians 6: light and darkness can never commune with one another.

The light that Paul is talking about is the Christian, as we are the "light of the world." The darkness is that of the world and ultimately our adversary, the Devil.

Many times we hear terms describing "Christian" activities and groups that are simply ungodly. In an effort to conceal their lusts for fleshly things, people will often attach the name of Christ to their worldly activities. This attachment eases the conscience and spiritualizes the action.

The flesh knows no end to our deceptive attitudes and disrespect to the Lord. Consider, for example, "Christian Rock" music. Christian is used to identify a follower of Christ while the word "rock" comes from the term "rock-n-roll." The very reason music was called "rock-n-roll" was because of the sexually rhythmic motions of the musicians performing, the driving beats, and response of the hearer [2].

While I do not believe that all contemporary Christian music is worldly and devilish, far too much is adequately called "rock-n-roll," as the musicians have unmistakably tried to look like, sound like, and act like the musicians of the world. However, we've pinned them "Christian" simply because they call themselves Christians and may make mention of some spiritual, albeit typically shallow, tone in their lyrics.

In the 1990s, members of the popular rock/grunge band Creed had to continuously make public statements informing their fans that they did not consider themselves a "Christian" band. The "Christian" label was given to them when several of their hit songs used spiritual sounding metaphors in their lyrics [3].

It makes no more sense to say "Christian rock" than to call a Budweiser "Christian beer" simply because the man drinking it calls himself a "Christian."

As a saved young man in the Navy, most of the time I was not serving God like I should have been. I can remember, on a few occasions, being in a bar and discussing the topic of God, religion, and even Jesus Christ. What a horrible testimony! I can affirm to you that it never helped me reach a lost person while I drank with him, even if I told him that I was a Christian.

What was once obvious to every believer, has now become a point of contention, yet Christians still are to look different, act different, and be different that the world.

In a world littered with "Christian" schools that are "Christian" in name only, to "Christian" music that satisfies the flesh more than glorifying Christ, we brand with a Christian label and call it good.

We have "Christian" comedy to appease our appetite for humor and even "Christian" dating services (which seems remarkably absurd). If you want a date, join a Bible-preaching, local church and learn to walk with God. When God sees that you are ready, He will bring the right person for you. The absurdity continues as one considers "Christian" night clubs, raves, and even "churches" offering group sessions in which members sit in a circle, smoke cigars, drink mixed cocktails, and talk about the Lord. These things are literally happening today. Something is wrong!

Paul says, "[…] and what communion hath light with darkness?" The answer to this question should be obvious to any true believer: "None!"

---

[1] Newport, Frank (25 December 2015). "Percentage of Christians in U.S. Drifting Down, but Still High." Gallup.

[2] Dictionary.com. "Why is it called "rock n' roll?" What does the "roll" mean?" http://www.disctionary.com/e/rock-and-roll/ (viewed November, 2018)

[3] Cummings, Tony (07 December 2004). "Scott Stapp: Ex-Creed man tells of his Christian conversion." www.crossrythms.co.uk

CHAPTER TWO

ARE YOU A CHRISTIAN?

In 2015, Gallup conducted a poll in which 75% of Americans questioned said they associated their religious belief with that of Christianity [1]. While this number has shifted downward from 84% just 15 years earlier, it remains a very surprising statistic to those who pay any attention to the current condition and deterioration of our society.

With a daily dose of pro-homosexuality shoved in the faces of Christians and hatred spewed toward any who dare believe in the biblical family model, it becomes rather difficult to understand where these numbers come from. All of this is capped with murder, violence, rioting, drunkenness, and a host of other evil imaginations practiced by a prophetic, end-time generation.

Things, however, become increasingly clearer when we find out that less than half of those polled, or 37%, actually attend any weekly religious services [2]. Further statistics tell us that only 3% of households tithe and less than 9% of born-again teenagers believe in moral absolutes.

Pick up any average household dictionary and search for the word "Christian." In it you will find a definition similar to the following: "someone who professes belief in Christianity or someone who follows the religion of Christ."

To this standard, the statistics we've just noted should come as no surprise. If a Christian is nothing more than someone who professes belief in a religion, then anyone can call themselves a Christian and live any way he or she desires. How sad our Savior must be at this undermining of His sacrifices.

The Biblical definition of a Christian, however, is far superior to anything you'll read in a typical dictionary.

What's In A Name?

"Wherefore God also hath highly exalted him, and given him a name which is above every name: that at the name of Jesus every knee should bow, of things in heaven, and things in earth, and things under the earth: And that every tongue should confess that Jesus Christ is Lord, to the glory of God the Father."

- Philippians 2:9-11

The Bible tells us that God has highly exalted His Son *"and given him a name which is above every name [...]"* That name is Jesus! The name Jesus means Savior. In The Greek it is Iesous, and in the Hebrew it is the name Yeshua.

Through time, man has used the name of Jesus in vanity and blasphemy; but one day every knee will bow and every tongue will confess Him. There can be no doubt that God is displeased by man's vulgarity. In fact, in Revelation 19:12 we find that God has given Jesus a name that *"no man knew, but He Himself."* It seems that God wants this new name to be unknown to man's vanity.

Jesus is also called Lord. In Revelation 19:16, we find that *"He hath on His vesture and on His thigh a name written, KING OF KINGS, AND LORD OF LORDS."* While in this passage Lord is referred to as His name, it is most often used as His position. Jesus is the KING of every king, and He is LORD of every lord.

Whereas His given name is Jesus and His position is Lord, we further learn that His title is Christ. Christ means "The Anointed One." It is His anointing blood that was shed to cover our sins. He is the Chosen, Anointed One.

Each of these names describes to us Who Jesus is: His name, Jesus (Savior), His position, Lord (Over All), and His title, Christ (The Anointed One).

This is similar to many areas of our lives. In the military for example, the Captain of a ship may be identified as follows: Captain (rank/title), John Smith (name), or Commanding Officer (position). Likewise the physician (position), Bob Johnson (name), is typically called Doctor (title).

In Philippians two, the Apostle Paul tells us that on that day, every soul will confess that Jesus the Savior, is Christ the Anointed One, and Lord over all.

So what's in a name? Does it really matter to God? In Proverbs 22:1 we read:

"A good name is rather to be chosen than great riches, and loving favour rather than silver and gold."

- Proverbs 22:1

Does God care how I use His Son's name when defining my lifestyle and activities? I believe, without question, that He does care; nevertheless I leave this question to the reader to determine how you may justify your usage of His name.

What Is A Biblical Christian?

We have previously noted how the world defines a Christian and now we will turn to the Word of God. After all, the Bible is to be our final authority in all matters.

The word "Christian" is found in the Bible only three times. Each of these usages are discovered in the New Testament: Acts 11:26, Acts 26:28, and I Peter 4:16.

Unlike the typical dictionary on your shelf, the Greek word "Christanos" literally means "a follower of Christ." At first glance, many would argue a case for simple semantics, but a simple Bible study proves otherwise. God tells us to "study to shew thyself approved unto God..." I submit that there is far more to being a follower of Christ than simply professing belief in Christianity. Being a Christian means to **follow** Christ! Further study in God's Word sheds more light on the subject.

The first mention of the word "Christian" is found in Acts 11:

*"And when he had found him, he brought him unto Antioch. And it came to pass, that a whole year they assembled themselves with the church, and taught much people. And the **disciples were called Christians** first at Antioch."*

- Acts 11:26

Many believe that the disciples were called Christians in a derogatory way by those who were persecuting the early church. The brand would have been used in a negative fashion as if to say, "You are nothing but little Christ."

Others believe that the name Christian was self-given to tell the world that they were followers of Christ. In either case, the important thing to notice is that only disciples of Jesus Christ were called Christians. In addition, these disciples seemed perfectly content being branded as such. Acts 11 shows us that in its most infant use of the title, a Christian was a disciple.

In both of the other instances that the word is used, they refer to the idea that disciples of Christ are Christians. In Acts 26:28, King Agrippa said, *"[...]*

almost thou persuadest me to be a Christian." Agrippa was telling Paul, "You have almost convinced me to be a follower of Christ."

Peter later affirms this principle as well:

"Yet if any man suffer as a Christian, let him not be ashamed…"

- I Peter 4:6

Jesus told His disciples, *"If the world hate you, ye know that it hated Me before it hated you."* Our Lord suffered great persecution and warns His followers that they would be hated and persecuted as well because they followed Him.

According to the Word of God, a Christian is a disciple of Christ. This was true during the time of the apostles and has not changed in the 21st century. Christians are not simply those who profess belief in Christ, but are disciples (followers) of Christ.

Imposter Disciples

Clearly the Scriptures reveal to us that in order to be a Christian you must be a disciple of Christ; however, not every disciple is a Christian.

If a disciple of Christ is someone who "follows" Christ, it may seem a little audacious to say some followers are not Christians, but this also is clearly taught in Scripture.

In John 6, Jesus had attracted a multitude of followers. Early in the chapter, we were witnesses of the feeding of the five thousand. This miracle was preceded by many others that had caused great intrigue on the part of the people. In response to the reception and persistency of the multitude, Jesus began to turn the context of the miracle into the spiritual realities of Himself: *"I am the bread of life [...]"*

While the people were fascinated with the miracles Jesus performed, they could not grasp the spiritual content of the Lord's Word. Disbelief led to murmuring and murmuring led to complete rejection of Christ. The Apostle Paul would make more sense of this for us when he stated *"But the natural man receiveth not the things of the Spirit of God: for they are foolishness unto him: neither can he know them, because they are spiritually discerned"* (I Corinthians 2:14).

Following this discourse, the Bible tells us in John 6:66, *"From that time many of His **disciples** went back, and walked no more with Him."* By divine revelation, John called them disciples; nevertheless, they did not believe. In fact, Jesus said in verse 64, *"But there are some of you that believe not [...]"*

Jesus would furthermore point out that even of the "chosen twelve" disciples, one of them was "a devil." Judas Iscariot (possessed by the Devil) was for three years, a follower of Christ- a disciple. He acted like, dressed like, and served like all the other disciples so much so that they never saw underneath his clever "costume" of discipleship. Like the multitude who walked away, Judas was an imposter.

Throughout our country and across the world, there are those who call themselves Christian. They by all appearances look like, act like, and sound like disciples of Christ. They may say all the right things and do all the right things, but before an All-knowing God they will be revealed as He says, "*I never knew you: depart from me, ye that work iniquity.*"

Of course, we speak of those who never come to a saving knowledge of Christ: they never accepted Jesus Christ as their personal Savior. Some may sit in Bible-believing churches, teach Sunday School classes, or even preach in pulpits, but their heart trusts in their own works and not in the finished work of Christ.

While there is no doubt there are those who claim to be followers, and those who even do follow, who are not true believers, is it possible to be a "born-again" believer, trusting fully in Christ for salvation, yet in all practical purposes still be an imposter Christian? I believe it is possible.

It is possible to know Christ as your Savior and not be a true follower or disciple. What is it then that makes a believer a true Christian? Rather, what are the characteristics of a true follower of Christ?

The "Real Deal"

Being a biblical Christian is not simply being saved. Biblical Christianity can be seen by others in the lives of those who demonstrate certain characteristics. This is not to suggest that someone who has been saved can lose their salvation. Once you are born again, you cannot be unborn again.

When a believer trusts Christ as their Savior, they are given eternal life. Eternal life begins the moment that one trusts Christ's substitutionary death on the cross for their sin. The very term "eternal," or "everlasting," proves that it will never end. Jesus said it this way:

"My sheep hear my voice, and I know them, and they follow me: And I give unto them eternal life; and they shall never perish, neither shall any man pluck them out of my hand. My Father, which gave them me, is greater than all; and no man is able to pluck them out of my Father's hand."

- John 10:27-29

The moment I trusted Christ as my Savior, I was saved and on my way to Heaven. There is no one, including myself, strong enough to take me away from the Lord: it is impossible. Yet, being saved, knowing I'm on my way to heaven, does not mean that my daily walk is one of following Christ. A Christian, however, is a follower of Christ.

At the age of nine years old, I attended a youth camp. After hearing a clear presentation of the Gospel, I accepted Christ as my personal Savior. By the time I entered high school, I began rebelling at home and school.

In 1995 at the tender age of seventeen, I joined the U.S. Navy. As I was stationed in various parts of the country and travelled the world, I began to backslide further and further from the Lord. I rarely attended church, only casually read my Bible, and prayed just when I needed God to do something. All of this time, I knew my salvation was secure in Christ and sealed by the Holy Spirit, yet I floundered (at best) in my walk with Christ.

The church which Christ loved and gave Himself for was not important enough for me to be involved in. The communication between Him and me was at a complete standstill except in those emergencies of life. No one could look at me and say, "Now, there's a Christian." Why? I was not acting like one, I did not look like one, and I certainly did not talk like one. I was still saved, and thank God I was, but on one else could see it. That is not being a follower of Christ; that is just "being."

True Christians--true followers-- are marked by their character. The "real deal" is easy to spot. A Christian reflects the glorious light of Jesus Christ in their daily life.

Most people can quickly identify a rose. While not all roses are exactly the same, their pedals, and the arrangement of their pedals are different from other flower. The rose is identified easily by its characteristic no matter what color they may be. Even when you may not visually spot it, your nose can often times tell when a bouquet is in the room.

Similarly, Christians who are the real deal will bear the marks of true Christianity just like a rose bears its unique marks. A true Christian will not be misidentified any sooner than a rose would be mistaken as a dandelion.

Are you bearing the marks and characteristics of a true follower of Christ? Are you the "real deal?" Are you a Christian?

---

[1] Newport, Frank (25 December 2015). "Percentage of Christians in U.S. Drifting Down, but Still High." Gallup.

[2] Religion: Gallup Historical Trends. www.Gallup.com. Gallup Inc.

CHAPTER THREE

A NEW BIRTH!

Christians are disciples of Christ, but what are the characteristics that define a true disciple? In Matthew chapters 4 and 5, we are introduced to the earliest recruiting of the disciples of Christ. Our first principle characteristic is found here:

"From that time Jesus began to preach and to say, Repent: for the kingdom of heaven is at hand."

- Matthew 4:17

Immediately following this verse we find that as Jesus walked by the Sea of Galilee, He called His first two disciples, Simon Peter and Andrew. While later in Scripture, we find out that each of the apostles were indeed saved and baptized under John the Baptist's ministry, Matthew 4:17 reminds us that Jesus' first concern was that His disciples were born-again believers.

"For the Son of man is come to seek and to save that which was lost."

- Luke 19:10

Everything Jesus did -- every miracle, every experience of physical healing, and every parable -- had at its foundation the priority of bringing souls to a saving knowledge of Him. Jesus's number one priority was to bring a sinful soul to repentance by revealing their sin and ultimately by providing salvation on the cross.

In John chapter 3, Jesus met with a Pharisee by the name of Nicodemus. Before Nicodemus could ask the question on his mind, Jesus answered it for him. The question was, "How can I get to heaven?" Jesus responded:

"Jesus answered and said unto him, Verily, verily, I say unto thee, Except a man be born again, he cannot see the kingdom of God."

- John 3:3

Jesus then explains to a perplexed Nicodemus that being born again is a spiritual birth that takes place when one puts their faith in the Son of God.

"That whosoever believeth in Him should not perish, but have eternal life. For God so loved the world, that He gave His only begotten Son, that whosoever believeth in Him should not perish, but have everlasting life."

- John 3:15-16

In these verses Jesus tells Nicodemus that an unbelieving man is lost in sin. Verse 18 reads, "*...he that believeth not is condemned already [...]*" What does this mean? An unbelieving man is condemned because of his sin. Paul tells us:

"For all have sinned and come short of the glory of God."

- Romans 3:23

"Wherefore, as by one man sin entered into the world, and death by sin: and so death passed upon all men, for all have sinned."

- Romans 5:12

Every one of us is a sinner because we are born "in sin:" it is part of our human nature. In fact, we commit sin because we are "in sin." As a result of Adam eating fruit of the Tree of the Knowledge of Good and Evil, sin came into the world. Every one of us are the seed of Adam and in our natural state we are sinners.

Sin means to "miss the mark." It is a violation of our actions, thoughts, and intents against the very glory and nature of God. As a result, there is a penalty (a price that must be paid) for it. The Bible tells us that this penalty is death:

"For the wages of sin is death…"

- Romans 6:23

No one can escape this penalty: it must be paid. The death spoken of is not just the end of our life on earth, but is also an eternal death. In fact, the Bible tells us of three different types of death: physical, spiritual, and eternal.

Physical death is the separation of the soul (inner man) from the body. We have all seen this at a funeral. The person's body is there, but you can no longer communicate with them. Why? Because the inner man (the conscience) is gone.

Spiritual death is the separation of God and man. Though we live physically when we are conceived, every one of us is spiritually dead at birth (Romans 5:12). In this natural state, man and God are at odds.

Have you ever read the Bible and didn't understand what it was saying? For the person who does not know Christ as their Savior, it is because God, the Author of the Bible, does not have a one-on-one relationship with you. God is alive, but if you are "dead," you cannot hear Him. Dead men do not hear the living.

The final death found in the Bible is Eternal Death. This, ultimately, is what Paul described in Romans 6:23, *"For the wages of sin is death."* It is also what Jesus told Nicodemus in John 3 when He used the word "perish." Eternal death is the separation of man from God for all eternity. There are only two places for man to spend eternity: the first is in Heaven with God and the other is in Hell and the Lake of Fire, separated from God. Notice Revelation 20:

"And the sea gave up the dead which were in it; and **death and hell** *delivered up* **the dead** *which were in them: and they were judged every man according to their works. And* **death and hell** *were cast into the lake of fire.* **This is the second death."**

- Revelation 20:13,14

This is what Jesus described to Nicodemus in John 3:18: *"...he that believeth not is condemned already."*

Heaven and Hell are two very literal places. The Bible tells us that because of our sin, we do not deserve to be in Heaven with Him; the only alternative is in Hell and ultimately the Lake of Fire.

God does not want that for you. In fact, this is the very reason He sent His only begotten Son, Jesus, into the world. Jesus's cry is to them and us, "Repent."

Repent means "to change one's mind." This changing of the mind leads to a change in direction. The Lord says that when you and I are convicted and recognize the fact that we are sinners heading toward eternal damnation, we are to repent (change our mind) of our sin and trust Him for a new direction.

This new direction is a new life in Christ. Lester Roloff said it this way, "Repentance is a godly sorrow for sin. Repentance is forsaking of sin. Real repentance is putting your trust in Jesus Christ so you will not live like that anymore."

"But God commendeth His love toward us, in that, while we were yet sinners, Christ died for us."

- Romans 5:8

Jesus paid the penalty of sin for you and me when He died on the cross. The moment that you recognize your condition in sin, realize the penalty for your sin, and trust in Jesus Christ to save you from your sin, you are born again.

The only difference between us and Nicodemus is that he was looking forward to Christ dying for him and you and I look back to Christ dying for us. The Apostle Paul says it this way:

"That if thou shalt confess with thy mouth the Lord Jesus, and shalt believe in thine heart that God hath raised Him from the dead, thou shalt be saved."

- Romans 10:9

"For whosoever shall call upon the name of the Lord shall be saved."

- Romans 10:13

The word "call" means "to make an appeal." When we recognize our condition and direction, we must *"call upon"* (make an appeal) to the Savior asking Him to save us from sin. The assurances of God's Word says that when we do that, *"thou shalt be saved."*

In fact, it is only by trusting Christ as a Savior that we can be saved. Buddha cannot save; Muhammed cannot save; the pope cannot save. Not a religion, a baptism or any measure of good works. Christ alone can save you from sin!

"Neither is there salvation in any other: for there is none other name under heaven given among men, whereby we must be saved."

- Acts 4:12

Jesus said it this way in John 14:6, *"I am **the way, the truth, and the life: no man cometh unto the Father but by me**."* Apart from accepting Jesus Christ as your personal Savior, there is **no** other way to get to Heaven. Again, Jesus told Nicodemus, "Ye must be born again."

A Christian is someone who, first and foremost, has accepted the gift of eternal life through Jesus Christ. To claim to be a follower of Christ and reject the payment that He made for you on the cross is both ludicrous and insulting to God. You may be able, like Judas, to hide the truth from everyone around you, but God knows if you're His child or not. If you are not, may I implore you to accept Christ as your personal Savior in this moment? Pray and ask Christ to save you. If you do, He will!

For many, you may not know what to ask in prayer. A true prayer will be what comes from your heart to His ears, and while a prayer itself will not save you, you may pray something like this:

"Dear Jesus, I know that I'm a sinner. I believe that because of sin, I am undeserving of Your gift. Yet your Bible tells me that You died on the cross for my sin and You rose again. I believe this is true and accept Your gift of salvation. Please, forgive me of my sin and help me to be what you desire for my life. Thank you Jesus, Amen."

If you have prayed that prayer, believing in your heart that Jesus would save you, then Jesus says that you shall *"not perish, but have everlasting life."* If you have just done that, that life begins this moment: nothing can ever change that! Let me encourage you to find a good, Bible-believing church in your area and begin living the life of a Christian.

CHAPTER FOUR

GROW UP!

Far too many believers are content to just coast through life. They beckon God only when they need something, they attend church services for no other purpose than to meet some need for easing the conscience, and they remain satisfied with never fulfilling the plan that God has for their life. This type of attitude is mediocrity at its finest. Churches are filled with immature Christians who are fit only to play with toys in the spiritual nursery.

This is not a condemnation of those who are recently saved, for their opportunities are just beginning, but this is rather a condemnation of those who, in many cases, have been saved for many years and sometimes, most of their lives. With great ease they could name the starting lineup of their favorite sports team, but think Moses, Elijah, and Jonah may very well be 3 of the 12 Apostles. Encourage one of the brethren? Forget it! These "diaper wearing" Christians are far too busy with the cares of this world.

Lack of knowledge is not the only clear indicator of the spiritually immature, in fact some things are far worse. Mr. or Miss "I've been in church my whole life so I know what to criticize" is certainly more discouraging. Pride, contentions, disregard for the lost, callousness, and the like, are clear indicators of believers who need to just grow up. Paul called it carnality.

"And I, brethren, could not speak unto you as unto spiritual, but as unto carnal, even as unto babes in Christ."

- I Corinthians 3:1

There is nothing sadder than seeing a "Christian," sometimes even a senior citizen, who has never grown up spiritually.

After salvation, spiritual growth is the most crucial characteristic of a Christian. Christ did not save you and then leave you on earth to continue to be what you've always been. A growing believer is a spiritually healthy Christian. In fact, brand new believers that are spiritually growing are healthier than the long-time Bible scholars who think they've grown to their full potential.

There is never a time in the life of a Christian when you're supposed to stop growing. The spiritually healthy Christian stops growing only after he has left this world and he has gone to Heaven. We often use the phrase, "he's graduated to Heaven," for the believer that has passed away and there is a certain Biblical truth to that.

As a pastor, it is usually evident which converts will potentially go on to live productive Christians lives and which will dwindle in the crowds. It often becomes evident in the first few weeks after their acceptance of Christ. This is not always the case, but typically the new convert who is hungry for more right away will be fed and growing. The same can be said for the person that has been saved for many years: are they hungry for more?

Spiritual Growth

After Jesus called the disciples in Matthew 4, we find them immediately under His teaching and preaching.

*"And going on from thence, he saw other two brethren, James the son of Zebedee, and John his brother, in a ship with Zebedee their Father, mending their nets, and he called to them. And they immediately left the ship and their father, and followed him. And Jesus went about all Galilee, **teaching** in their synagogues, and **preaching** the gospel of the kingdom…"*

- Matthew 4:21-23

*"And seeing the multitudes, He went up into a mountain: and when He was set, His disciples came unto Him: And He opened His mouth, and **taught** them…"*

- Matthew 5:1-2

Why would Jesus immediately begin teaching the people? Simple: He wanted them to immediately begin growing. He wants the new believer today to immediately begin to grow spiritually as well.

Not only are new believers instructed to grow, but those who've been saved for many years should be ever seeking new fruit and growth in their own lives. After nearly three years of these disciples following Christ, Jesus told them in John 16, "I will send the Comforter (the Holy Spirit), And when He comes," *"…He will guide you into all truth[…]"* (John 16:13). In fact, Jesus had just finished telling the disciples, *"I have yet many things to say unto you, but ye cannot bear them now"* (John 16:12). It is impossible for you to get everything He wants you to know in a short time. It will take you a lifetime of experience and growth to blossom into what He wants for you. Peter exhorts this way:

"But grow in grace, and in the knowledge of our Lord and Savior Jesus Christ. To Him be glory both now and for ever. Amen."

- II Peter 3:18

Whether you've just trusted Christ as your Savior, or you've been saved for many years but have never seen real fruit in your Christian walk, the following principles are Scriptural steps for early growth.

Baptism

The first step of growth for the new believer is that of Scriptural baptism. Baptism is the outward picture of what has already happened on the inside when you were saved. It is a picture of the death, burial, and resurrection of Jesus Christ and it demonstrates in the physical realm what your heart has believed.

"They that gladly received his word were baptized[...]"

- Acts 2:41

In addition, baptism tells others that we identify ourselves with Christ. Our old sin nature is buried in the likeness of His death and our new Christ-like nature is raised to walk in the newness of the born-again life.

"But when they believed Philip preaching the things concerning the kingdom of God, and the name of Jesus Christ, they were baptized, both men and women."

- Acts 8:12

Baptism is always the very first step of obedience as a new believer. Baptism is not salvation, but rather it accompanies salvation. This is much like how a ring on the finger is not marriage, but it shows the world that I am married, that I am committed to my wife, and she is committed to me. Baptism is a symbol -- a picture.

Many teach that baptism is part of or is the method by which we are saved. This type of teaching is both biblically inaccurate and dangerous. This is dangerous because it leaves many people thinking that they are on their way to heaven, having been baptized, but they are not. Salvation, as previously noted, comes only through accepting Christ as your Savior. Notice the following:

"And he said unto Jesus, Lord, remember me when thou comest into Thy kingdom. And Jesus said unto him, Verily I say unto thee, Today shalt thou be with Me in paradise."

- Luke 23:42-43

This conversation took place between Jesus and one of the thieves on the cross next to Him during the crucifixion. If baptism were necessary for salvation, Jesus would not have said to the thief, you will *"be with me in paradise."* Jesus knew this man would not live long enough to be able to get baptized nor would he have the opportunity.

WHAT'S KEEPING YOU?

Not only do some erroneously believe baptism will earn them a way to heaven, but another group refuses altogether to be baptized. As a pastor I have heard many reasons why someone will not get baptized:

Fear

Some choose not to be baptized for fear of what others might think. Jesus warns us of the need to overcome this fear.

"Whosoever therefore shall confess Me before men, him will I confess before My Father which is in heaven."

- Matthew 10:32

Fear should never keep us from doing God's will. In fact, fear will only keep you from being the Christian God wants you to be.

Misunderstanding

I have seen many people who have recently accepted Christ refuse baptism because they were already "baptized," possibly as a child or in another church. As noted earlier, Biblical baptism can only take place after you've accepted Christ as your Savior. How can one identify with Christ when they've never accepted Him as Savior? You can't.

In every example in the Bible of baptism, apart from Jesus Himself, people went into the water only after they were saved. If you were "baptized" before you were saved, whether as a child or to join some "church," then according to the Bible, you were not baptized. You only got wet: that's all.

Commitment

In many instances, people will refuse to be baptized because, unlike salvation, it makes them feel the need to be more committed. If commitment scares you, then you don't really want to be a Christian anyway. The Christian life is a life of dedication and commitment to the things of Christ. A lack of commitment will spiritually cripple a believer. It will keep you from ever being what Jesus wants you to be, or doing what He wants you to do.

"And whosoever doth not bear his cross, and come after me, cannot be my disciple."

- Luke 14:27

WHAT'S CRIPPLING YOU?

I have three sons. I can recall being in the delivery room when all three were born. The very first thing that concerned the nurses and doctors was that the airway of the baby was clear and the sound of crying came out of their little mouths. This sent the signal to the doctor present that the baby's lungs were operating as they should and that there were no immediate complications.

Before my wife and I could hold any one of them, before she could feed them, before anything, this needed to happen. If one of my sons, when born, would not have been able to breathe and was unable to survive, it would not have changed the fact that they were born. It would only change that he could have never grown.

This is much the same with a new Christian. If a new believer chooses not to be baptized, it does not change the fact that they were born-again. However, it does mean that they will struggle to be fed, causing them to never grow in the knowledge of Christ and in the things of Him.

Sadly, many believers are spiritually crippled by their choice not to be baptized. I have seen it multiple times: a believer who swears they love the Lord remains stunted in their spiritual growth because they refuse to follow the Lord in believers' baptism. Unwilling to follow Christ's obvious will, why would they ever follow Him in any other area?

Church Membership

Much like baptism, joining a local church is considered by many to be a tough decision. Home-based Bible studies, progressive church hopping, and "churches" without membership are becoming more and more popular in our society. Many stay home altogether, justifying their sin by saying, "I don't need to be in church to believe." Some clarify, "I get my church on T.V. or through the internet."

While it is true that someone does not need to be in church to be a believer, a logically simple Bible study proves that in order to be a Christian (a true disciple), you must be a member of a local Bible-believing church. The following three reasons bring us to this conclusion:

CHRIST ESTABLISHED THE CHURCH

God established three social institutions. The government (Genesis 19, Romans 13:1-2), the home (Genesis 2:18-25), and the church (Matthew 16:18). The success or failure of each of these institutions directly affects the others. What do we mean? When homes (families) are weak, churches will struggle. When churches are weak, the home will typically struggle. When governments levy attacks on either the home or the church, struggles will follow.

For example, this is becoming increasingly clear as the homosexual agenda has risen in popularity.

Homosexuality destroys the image of the home that God has created. The redefining of the institution of marriage has impacted governments around the world. As the government has legislated harsher penalties in the name of political correctness, a great many churches have now begun to accept what God calls an abomination. This single illustration is what we mean when we say that the failure in one institution will impact the other institutions.

The point is that the Christian that abandons the church will struggle in their home (in marriages, relationships with children/parents, etc.).

Church is for your good. Like the home, the church was established by God. More directly, the church was established by Christ. In Matthew 16:18, Jesus said, *"...upon this rock I will build My church;..."* Christ would not have established the local church if it was not important for His followers to be a part of the local church.

CHRIST LOVED THE CHURCH

"Husbands, love your wives, even as Christ also loved the church, and gave Himself for it[...]"

- Ephesians 5:25

Jesus loved the church enough to give His life for it. Imagine the audacity of the believer who boldly claims "I love Jesus," but fails to love and cherish the very thing that He loved. If someone refuses to be a part of what He gave himself for, then he or she is obviously not a follower of Christ.

CHRIST CHOSE THE CHURCH

When giving the Great Commission, Jesus gave the church a threefold job.

"And Jesus came and spake unto them, saying, All power is given unto Me in heaven and in earth. Go ye therefore, and teach all nations, baptizing them in the name of the Father, and of the Son, and of the Holy Ghost: Teaching them to observe all things whatsoever I have commanded you; and, lo, I am with you alway, even unto the end of the world. Amen."

- Matthew 28:18-20

With this three-fold commission, Jesus gave the marching orders to the local New Testament church: teach all nations (make disciples), baptize (include disciples), and teach them (disciple disciples).

The responsibility of the home is to *"be fruitful, and multiply."* Along with this initial command, given to Adam and Eve in Genesis 1, additional instructions are given throughout the revelation of Scripture: *"Train up a child," "teach your children,"* and other similar commands are given throughout the Bible.

Likewise, the church has been given similar instructions. The church is to teach all nations, or multiply, and follow that by "teaching the things you've learned of me."

Christ chose the church to be the place where believers are taught the Word of God.

"Take heed therefore unto yourselves, and to all the flock, over the which the Holy Ghost hath made you overseers, to feed the church of God, which He hath purchased with His own blood."

- Acts 20:28

This charge is given to the pastor. The pastor's instruction is to feed God's people His Word. If you were a shepherd of sheep and each day you went out to feed the sheep, but one would not come in at feeding time, it would not take long to notice the lack of growth. The same is true with the believer. If you choose not to come into the church to receive the spiritual food that God has prepared for you, you will not grow like you should.

"Not forsaking the assembling of ourselves together, as the manner of some is; but exhorting one another: and so much the more, as ye see the day approaching."

- Hebrews 10:25

God puts a direct emphasis on the attendance of His church. Why? Because God wants you to grow and to grow properly, you must be fed.

Fellowship With God

"But grow in grace, and in the knowledge of our Lord and Savior Jesus Christ. To Him be glory both now and for ever. Amen."

- II Peter 3:18

The Bible teaches us the principle of growing in grace. "But if grace is free," someone might ask, "how can I grow in it?" The answer is simple: grace is God giving to you and me what we do not deserve. It is free. This is why the Bible does not say, "grow toward grace." Once you and I have received grace, we are to grow in it.

While God's grace is given at salvation, it is also God's grace that enables me to live for Him daily. It is through His grace that I can accomplish that which He calls me to do.

In addition, we are to grow in the knowledge of our Lord and Savior Jesus Christ. The knowledge we grow in is not just a "knowing about," but rather a "knowing Him." The only way we can know Him more is through fellowship.

My wife and I have been married now for 18 years. When we first met, we both wanted to spend as much time with each other as possible. I wanted to know everything about her. After months of quality time spent together, when we married I still knew only a little about her. It has taken 18 years of daily fellowship and companionship to know her like I do today and still we learn and grow closer together each day. Just about the time I think I know everything about her, I learn something new.

The same is true in the Christian's life. The Lord wants to fellowship with His followers every day. His desire for you and me is that through continuous fellowship, we will grow in our knowledge of Him: we should not just know about Him, but we should know Him.

As you study the gospels, you will find a group of disciples that gave everything to spend time with Jesus. These disciples were continuously taught more and more about their Savior. They broke bread with Him, they observed Him, and they regularly asked questions of Him. After three years of following closely, they never stopped learning from Him. Through continuous conversation and fellowship, they grew to know Him more.

BIBLE READING

We, as disciples, may no longer be able to converse with the Lord face-to-face, we are not able to hear His audible voice like they could, but we can still fellowship. God has given us the revelation of Himself through the Bible. It is through His Word that He communicates with you and me.

"Search the scriptures; for in them ye think ye have eternal life: and they are they which testify of Me."

- John 5:39

Jesus tells us that the Scriptures are a testimony of Himself. It is impossible for the believer to know Christ intimately without opening, reading, and studying the Bible.

PRAYER

Through reading and studying of the Bible, we are touched with the Words of our Savior, but fellowship is more than just reading your Bible. God desires to hear from us as well. Prayer is the avenue through which we talk to God.

For many Christians, prayer is some sort of formal "speech," given with our heads bowed and eyes closed, built upon the best oracle dialogue we can muster. While there may be a time and place for such formality, true fellowshipping prayer comes from the heart of the sheep to the ears of the Shepherd. In Romans 8, Paul said, *"Whereby we cry, Abba, Father."* Your Father wants to fellowship with you.

Prayer is not just approaching God with some laundry list of needs: it is fellowship. When I spend time in conversation with my wife, I don't just tell her all my needs: I tell her my heart. I tell her how much I adore her, I tell her what I love about her, I ask her what I can do for her. I fellowship with my wife through conversation and our prayer time should be the same with God.

Listed below are a few biblical principles of prayer:

<u>Pray in a designated time and place</u> (Luke 11:1-2). Jesus said, *"when ye pray [...]"* It is wise to have a dedicated time and a quiet place to pray.

<u>Pray always</u> (I Thessalonians 5:17). While we should have a designated time to pray, our fellowship with Him should never cease.

<u>Pray fervently</u> (James 5:16). Sadly, too many of our prayers are shallow and weak. It is no wonder we expect God not to hear us. Pray fervently.

<u>Pray expectantly</u> (Matthew 17:20-21, Hebrews 11:6). It is impossible to please God without faith. Our prayers should be bathed in the belief that God will accomplish His will.

<u>Pray boldly</u> (Hebrews 4:16). Because of the blood of Jesus Christ, we have direct access to God the Father. Boldness is not based upon our accomplishments, but His!

<u>Pray humbly</u> (Luke 11:2). This may seem to directly contradict the previous statement, but we mean that we should pray honoring Him. Our access to His throne room should lift Him high (*"Hallowed be thy name [...]"*) and force us prostrate before Him.

<u>Pray sacrificially</u> (Luke 11:2). Too many prayers are based upon "what I can get," rather than "what can I give." Jesus said, *"Thy will be done[...]"* Our prayer should be, "Lord, how can you use me?" In addition, James 5:15-16 reminds us to pray for others.

When your eyes are closed or open: pray. When you are kneeling or driving: pray. Before and during a meal: pray. At an altar and in the park: pray. Prayer is a privileged opportunity to fellowship with Him.

STRIVING TO KNOW HIM

The Apostle Paul is often described as one of the greatest Christians to have lived. As you study his life, you will quickly notice that he never stopped spending time with God. Why? Paul, like any true Christian, understood that growing in grace and in knowledge never ceases in this life. Notice his testimony:

"Yea doubtless, and I count all things but loss for **the excellency of the knowledge of Christ Jesus my Lord**: *for whom I have suffered the loss of all things, and do count them but dung, that I may win Christ [...]"*

- Philippians 3:8

Paul continues:

*"**That I may know Him**, and the power of His resurrection, and the fellowship of His sufferings, being made conformable unto his death [...]"*

- Philippians 3:10

Paul's greatest desire was to know Christ. Past achievements meant nothing: "That I may know Him," he says!

A true Christ follower constantly longs to know Christ more. A Christian daily spends time in fellowship with their Savior. Far too many Christians are "used-to" Christians. Christianity is not about what you used to do, but about Who you walk with every day!

CHAPTER FIVE

SHINE!

The title of this book is "Shine!" I believe that is one of the themes of the Christian life- we are to let our lives shine to a lost world.

The Gospel of John begins with the following revealing phrase;

"In Him was life; and the life was the light of men. And the light shineth in darkness; and the darkness comprehended it not [...] That was the true Light, which lighteth every man that cometh into the world."

- John 1:4-5,9

Jesus is the Light of the world; our sin is revealed through the light of His Word. Our salvation is revealed through the light of His sacrifice. He is not a light: He is The Light!

In Christ, the believer is instructed throughout the New Testament to walk in the light (I John 1:7), love the light (John 3:19), and to shine the light (Matthew 5:16). In Christ, the believer has within in himself the Light of Jesus Christ and we are called to shine!

"Then spake Jesus again unto them, saying, I am the light of the world: he that followeth me shall not walk in darkness, but shall have the light of life."

- John 8:12

Shine in Difficulties

"Rejoice, and be exceeding glad: for great is your reward in heaven: for so persecuted they the prophets which were before you. Ye are the salt of the earth: but if the salt have lost his savour, wherewith shall it be salted? It is thenceforth good for nothing, but to be cast out, and to be trodden under foot of men. Ye are the light of the world. A city that is set on an hill cannot be hid. Neither do men light a candle, and put it under a bushel, but on a candlestick; and it giveth light unto all that are in the house. Let your light so shine before men, that they may see your good works, and glorify your Father which is in heaven."

- Matthew 5:12-16

Sit in almost any church long enough and you will undoubtedly hear a message preached on this very text. Then why are so many "Christians" moping their way through life? They're happy when the blessings are coming in, but they're miserable at the first sign of troubled waters. This is not a Christ-like attitude.

Notice again: Jesus says, *"Rejoice, and be exceeding glad: for great is your reward in heaven: for so persecuted they the prophets which were before you."* Just prior to this statement, Jesus had given His disciples what we usually call the Blessed Beatitudes. *"Blessed are the poor in spirit[...]" "Blessed are they that mourn[...]"* Jesus even said, *"Blessed are they which are persecuted."* He followed this by reminding them to *"Rejoice!"*

"Lord, how can I rejoice when I am poor in spirit or even when I am being persecuted?" He responded, *"for great is your reward[...]"*

On your worst day, you can still rejoice. How? Your reward is in Heaven! I am reminded of a familiar saying, "The worst thing that can happen to you and me is that we die and go to Heaven." That is worth rejoicing over. In fact, the word "blessed" means happy or well off. If you're saved, no matter what is going on around you, you are blessed and can rejoice!

Several years ago I attended a funeral for the daughter of a missionary family who served in Cambodia. Toward the end of the service, the father of this precious two-year-old girl, who had abruptly died after acquiring an illness, got up and gave a testimony of her life. Through tears, the courageous father repeated over and over how good God is. He meant every word: God is good! This is the type of testimony every true Christian should have. It does not take away the pain of the situation; nevertheless, God is still good!

A very common misconception among believers is that joy means happiness. Look again at the words of our Savior: *"Blessed are they that mourn[...]"*

A person mourning the loss of a loved one is not happy in the moment, yet Jesus says they can still rejoice. They can rejoice knowing that though they will not see their loved one again on this earth, they will see their loved one again in Heaven. They can rejoice knowing that their Comforter knows what it is like to the lose someone He loves. Some might say, "Oh Lazarus." Yes, but even more than that. Jesus lost every one of those disciples who would not believe (John 6) and He loses each person who rejects Him today as well. What was His response? He rejoiced in those who did not leave. His light continued to shine.

As Stephen stood before the council that would stone him to death, we are witness to a man who shined in difficulty.

"And all that sat in the council, looking stedfastly on him, saw his face as it had been the face of an angel."

- Acts 6:15

On trial and faced with the harshest of penalties for nothing more than preaching, Stephen shined his light so brightly that the council could not believe what they were seeing.

The next few verses record the final moments of Stephen's life. Was it a happy time for Stephen? No. Yet he knew, *"Blessed are they which are persecuted for righteousness' sake."*

Happiness looks at our circumstances. It is the response of viewing the surroundings. Joy, or rejoicing, looks beyond those circumstances to the end result. Joy considers within its prism how God will be glorified, how wrongs will be made right, and how true rewards will be coming. Once again we look to Christ Himself…He is our greatest example.

*"Looking unto Jesus, the author and finisher of our faith; who **for the joy that was set before Him** endured the cross, despising the shame, and is set down at the right hand of the throne of God."*

- Hebrews 12:2

The very next verse exhorts you and me to put our struggles in view of this truth:

*"**For consider him** that endured such contradiction of sinners against himself, **lest ye be wearied and faint** in your minds."*

- Hebrews 12:3

There was no pleasure— nothing worthy of happiness— in Jesus going to the cross, yet the Bible clearly states that He viewed the *"joy that was set before Him [...]"* The writer continues and reminds us that when you struggle to trust Him by faith, consider that Christ rejoiced on the cross.

How could He rejoice while enduring His death on the cross? Jesus saw your salvation and my salvation beyond the lens of His suffering. Consider that when you are in troubled waters. Consider Him!

It is my prayer that more Christians would live by this principle: your life is meant to be a radiant one. God never promises a problem-free life, and in fact, we have quite the opposite. This world is not under the control of you and me, but rather is under the control of Satan. Satan does not want you to live happy as a Christ follower and he seeks to destroy you.

The life of Job highlights this principle. After losing all of his sons, daughters, riches, and health, Job still shined his light.

"...Naked came I out of my mother's womb, and naked shall I return thither: the Lord gave, and the Lord hath taken away; **blessed be the name of the Lord.***"*

- Job 1:21

If God could give Job the strength to rejoice in Him after losing so much, then God is big enough to give me strength to rejoice when I do not get my way, or when I just got laid off from work, or when someone was unfriendly to me at church.

Christian, how are you at rejoicing? Do you still shine when trouble comes or is the wick of your candle dampened by the wax of sorrow? Shine in difficulties.

Shine in Daily Living

"Let your light so shine before men, that they may see your good works, ad glorify your Father which is in heaven."

- Matthew 5:16

As you consider the life of Jesus, it is remarkable to discover that even in the midst of persecution, He shined. One may argue, "That's not remarkable: He is

God and we should expect such." While you and I are not perfect like Christ is, we do gain from His example and strength, and we are likewise called to shine in trouble.

In Matthew 5, however, the context tells us the importance of not only shining in persecution, but shining always. Jesus teaches us in this passage to be different than the world, not just when trouble comes, not just when things are good, but in every way and in every day.

"Ye are the salt of the earth: but if the salt have lost his savour, wherewith shall it be salted? It is henceforth good for nothing, but to be cast out, and to be trodden under foot of men."

- Matthew 5:13

The Creator, Jesus, beautifully applies an element of His creation to illustrate what a Christian ought to be. *"Ye are the salt[...]"* Salt is known to have over 14,000 uses, but is generally recognized for its 4 following characteristics: it penetrates, it cleanses, it purifies, and it preserves.

The Christian carries within themselves the knowledge of the gospel. The gospel has the power to penetrate the life of a sinner and bring them to repentance. Jesus states that it is possible, however, for salt to lose its savor. In other words, it no longer has its tang. A Christian who refuses to take the penetrating power of the gospel to the lost is like salt that has lost its tang.

Salt is also used to cleanse. If you were to take the time to study the uses of salt, you would find that there is an abundance of cleansing possibilities. The average American home spends countless dollars buying cleaning agents to use around the home, but in many cases salt and water would do a better job. One example is in the tub. The right mixture of salt and water can clean a tub quicker and better than most store-bought cleaners.

Jesus says that because we are Christians, we are the salt of the earth. We do not necessarily need politicians to pass laws to protect the true meaning of marriage; we just need Christians to be salty! We do not necessarily need employers to make rules in the work place against profanity; we just need Christians to be salty! The problem today is that Christians have ceased to be salty.

When Christians cease to be salty, Jesus says, "*It is thenceforth good for nothing, but to be cast out, and to be trodden under foot of men.*" In the biblical days of unpaved streets, potholes were a damaging burden to the wagons and carts of travelers. Often, salt that lost its savor would be used to fill those potholes because it had no other particular use. It would be trodden under the foot of men.

Far too many "Christians" have rendered themselves useless for the purposes that God intended them. There may still be a use for them, but it is not how God planned. True Christians have savor to them; true

Christians shine brightly. Their testimony is used by God to bring glory upon Himself.

We teach our children to sing, "This little light of mine, I'm going to let it shine." It needs to be far more than a simple melody sung in a classroom, it should be our goal in life.

Our conversation (lifestyle) is to be of Heaven, not of this earth. If you live a life for Christ, you may hear some who will criticize and mock your lifestyle, they did the same thing to our Savior, but as He did, we are to shine.

The earliest Christians were called "little Christs" for a reason. They determined to be Christ-like, and I believe they wore the title as a badge of honor. Will you do the same? The Christian life is not about you: your light is to shine so that the world will see you and *"glorify your Father which is in heaven."*

CHAPTER SIX

BE PECULIAR!

In the previous chapter, you were introduced to passages of Scripture that remind us of the importance of shining our light. It is impossible to shine the light of Jesus Christ when we look like, act like, and sound like the world. "While Christians are in this world, they are not of this world according to Jesus (John 15 and John 17:15-16).

The Bible word used to describe being in this world but not of this world is sanctification. Sanctification means "to be separated." As Christians, we are to be unique from the world, different, or as Peter said, *"a peculiar people"* (I Peter 2:9). Some might find these terms uncomfortable as they assume God calls us to be weird. In fact, many dedicated Christians feel it is important to do just that… but that is not necessarily what sanctification is about.

Part of the believer's sanctification is modesty. Modesty is the opposite of pride; modesty does not call attention to ourselves. An unbalanced Christian, struggling to maintain modesty, can oftentimes bring the very undue attention upon themselves that they so strongly oppose and sought to avoid. Christians are peculiar, not because we try to be, but rather because He makes us such.

Sanctification is His working in us to change us into the very image of His son. This process takes place on the inside and works its way out. Sadly, too many try to reverse the process.

In an effort to be so different from the unsaved, many Christians fall into traps of arrogance and pride, and can often be viewed as unapproachable and haughty. The Pharisees of the New Testament, albeit unsaved, acted this way. The Apostle Paul addressed those who showed pretense and also reprimanded those who arrogantly argued their differences. This is not Biblical sanctification.

Biblical sanctification is not me working on me to change: it is Him working on me as I surrender to Him. It is also not being weird, unapproachable, or showmanship; sanctification is being set apart; it is being different like Christ was different.

With this definition in mind, the Bible reveals to us several areas of the Christian life in which we should be different. As we learn to yield ourselves to the Holy Spirit within us, He will work from the inside out.

SPEECH

Our speech should be filled with grace and *"seasoned with salt."*

"Let your speech be alway with grace, seasoned with salt, that ye may know how ye ought to answer every man."

- Colossians 4:6

The Christian is someone whose speech builds up others: their words do not tear others down. Far too many overbearing loudmouths spend every social media post, every family gathering, or (sadly) many preaching opportunities tearing down others. I believe in following the leading of the Holy Spirit, I adamantly believe in preaching "Thus saith the Lord," but we would do well to make sure our speech is filled with grace. It should be, "Thus saith the Lord," and not, "Thus saith me."

Likewise, our speech should bring honor, not reproach, to Jesus Christ.

*"And **whatsoever ye do in word** or deed, do all in the name of the Lord Jesus, giving thanks to God and the Father by Him."*

- Colossians 3:17

For every word you speak, you will give an account (Matthew 12:36); be very mindful about what you speak. Our children sing the song, "Oh be careful little mouth what you say."

Your speech, however, will not change if your heart is not first changed.

"O generation of vipers, how can ye, being evil, speak good things? for out of the abundance of the heart, the mouth speaketh."

- Matthew 12:34

As you allow Christ to work in you and through you, your speech should change. This is the process of continued sanctification. The "Christian" who has no control over their tongue is one who is not being changed.

BEHAVIOR

Behavior speaks of our conduct and our bearing. It is control over our actions and reactions. Our behavior also considers our daily disposition in front to others. On multiple occasions, Paul addressed the behavior of Christians. One example can be found in Ephesians:

"Wherefore putting away lying, speak every man truth with his neighbor: or we are members one of another. Be ye angry, and sin not: let not the sun go down upon your wrath: Neither give place to the devil."

- Ephesians 4:25-27

Paul continued:

"Let all bitterness, and wrath, and anger, and clamour, and evil speaking, be put away from you, with all malice: And be ye kind one to another, tenderhearted, forgiving one another, even as God for Christ's sake hath forgiven you."

- Ephesians 4:31-32

A Christian who has no control over their behavior is no Christ-follower at all. Jesus stated as much:

"Herein is my Father glorified, that ye bear much fruit; **so shall ye be my disciples.** *As the Father hath loved me, so have I loved you:* **continue ye in my love.**"

- John 15:8-9

The behavior we have toward others is a clear indication of where we are in our Christian lives. Someone who struggles to love others behaves in ways that are unbecoming to a Christian. Again, Jesus said:

"A new commandment I give unto you, That ye love one another; as I have loved you, that ye also love one another. **By this shall all men know that ye are my disciples, if ye have love one to another.**"

- John 13:34-35

ACTIONS

While behavior is often based on our reactions, a Christian's daily actions are just as important. Jesus said, *"Let your light so shine before men, that* **they may see your good works***, and glorify your Father which is in Heaven"* (Matthew 5:16).

In Ephesians 2, Paul reminded us that we are not saved by our works, but we are most certainly sanctified unto good works:

"For by grace are ye saved through faith; and that not of yourselves: it is the gift of God: Not of works, lest any man should boast. For we are His workmanship, **created in**

Christ Jesus unto good works*, which God hath before ordained that we should walk in them."*

- Ephesians 2:8-10

Contrary to the shady teaching of the casual, contemporary Christian, the things that we do matter. They don't matter **for** salvation, but **because** of salvation.

DRESS

Nowhere in Scripture are we told specifically what men and women are supposed to wear. Any honest student knows that there are shifts in cultures, demographics, and generations that all impact what we wear. However, the Bible does speak of clothing in two ways: modesty and distinction.

As stated previously, modesty is the opposite of pride. In 1 Timothy, Paul addressed modesty for women when he said, *"In like manner also, that women adorn themselves in modest apparel [...]"* (I Timothy 2:9). While many have speculated what type of clothing this exactly means, and even argue to the point, I firmly believe it is a matter of jurisdiction. It is a father's, husband's, and pastor's responsibility (as jurisdiction applies) to determine what exactly this means as God leads them. But modesty does matter!

Modesty does not just apply to women. While it is explicitly stated that women are to dress modestly, men are also to make every attempt to be modest. If you are saved, your body is not yours to do what you want with. First, it belongs to the Holy Spirit. It is His Temple (I Corinthians 6:19). Second, if you are married, your body belongs to your spouse (I Corinthians 7:4). Both men and women are accountable to God and your spouse to be modest.

The other area of clothing implied in Scripture is in the area of distinction. Again, I Timothy explicitly addressed women's apparel; therefore, it implied it is different from men's apparel. This is the case throughout Scripture: men and women should look different. While the world may be confused about the differences between men and women, a born-again Christian should not be. Men should look like men and women should look like women. To what extent this principle is applied, I yield again to jurisdiction, but there should be no question that God cares about distinction.

Also, Christians should be distinctly and appropriately dressed in any activity. What do we mean? I believe that Christians should be distinct when they go out by being dressed appropriately for varying occasions. When you go to church to worship, you should dress like you're going to church and not dress like you're going to soccer practice. When you go to the grocery store, you should dress appropriately and not dress like you're going to bed. While it may not always be within our capabilities to do so, we should strive to make the effort to be distinct. This may primarily be an opinion, but in my experience the world notices whether a person dresses distinctly or not.

While I feel much more could be said in the practical applications of sanctification, it is not the intent of this book to address them all. The Bible should be our final authority for all matters of practice and I encourage the reader to study the importance of such topics. Just remember: Christians are to be peculiar, different, and sanctified.

CHAPTER SEVEN

GET BUSY!

In early 2003, while still serving in the Navy, I was sent out on a detachment to Miramar Marine Station in the San Diego area. I found a good, Bible-believing church to attend while I was there. I called the director of the military ministry and asked for transportation to church.

I remember asking my driver if he was involved in full-time ministry. His answer was, "Yes." Later in the conversation, the man began telling me about his job, which was not as a staff member of the church. I asked the man, "I thought you were in full-time ministry?" In response to my question, my driver smiled and began to explain, "Every Christian is supposed to be involved in full-time service to our Lord. Sure, I have a job that pays the bills, but I serve Him full-time."

I had never thought of my Christian life in that way before, yet the more I study the Bible, the more I have to agree with the man. Christian, either you are in full-time ministry or you are not a Christian.

We often think of the pastor, youth pastor, or music minister as the only full-time servants of God, but every Christian is called to serve God full-time. Everything else is second to that service. Your job (where you earn your paycheck) should have little to no bearing on your service to Him that you claim to follow. Notice the reaction of Jesus's disciples when He called them:

"And Jesus, walking by the sea of Galilee, saw two brethren, Simon called Peter, and Andrew his brother, casting a net into the sea: for they were fishers. And he saith unto them, Follow Me, and I will make you fishers of men. And they straightway left their nets, and followed him."

- Matthew 4:18-20

Consider a couple things about this call. First, some might argue that this is a call to just future apostles and pastors. While that is true, this is first a call to become disciples. A disciple is a follower of Christ and a follower of Christ is a Christian. Christian, Christ has called every one of us to follow Him and be made *"fishers of men."*

Second, these men were not hired by Jesus. They did not begin to draw a full-time salary with benefits and pensions for following Jesus. This was not the last time they would ever fish, but they became disciples because they followed Him and following Him made them full-time servants. God may not call you to leave your job and become a pastor, missionary, or church secretary, but you are called to serve Him. Every job (that which pays the bills), whether it is a pastoral position, a Christian school teacher, or a waiter serving tables is a blessing of resources for you to adequately serve your Savior in the way He calls you. The job itself should always be second to His calling. It is a means to an end and it not the definition of who you are.

After planting and pastoring two churches, I know all too well the difficulty of working a full-time job, maintaining the right relationships with my family, and serving God full-time. Yet every time I have worked a secular job to pay the bills, God has given me the strength and aptitude to accomplish what He's called me to do.

I also know all too well some of the pathetic excuses "Christians" use to not serve, to not be faithful, and to not be disciples. Christians are called to serve. Get busy! God has given you a spiritual gift to exercise within the local church…use it!

Notice, as we continue, what happened next:

"And going on from thence, He saw other two brethren, James the son of Zebedee, and John his brother [...] and He called them. And they immediately left the ship and their father, and followed Him. And Jesus went about all Galilee, teaching in their synagogues, and preaching the gospel of the kingdom [...]"

- Matthew 4:21-23

In addition to the call to serve, these disciples left their professions to hear Him preach and teach. If you choose not to be where the teaching and the preaching of God's Word is taking place, then it is not fair to call yourself a disciple like these men did. If your football game is more important than being in church, then you are not a Christian. If your hunting excursion keeps you from hearing the preaching, then you are not a Christ-follower.

It is not my intention to advocate that it is never excusable to be out of church, to never take a vacation, or to sit through a service when one is miserably sick, but church attendance should be one of your greatest priorities if you are a Christian.

"And let us consider one another to provoke unto love and to good works: Not forsaking the assembling of ourselves together, as the manner of some is; but exhorting one another; and so much the more, as ye see the day approaching."

- Hebrews 10:24-25

A true Christ-follower would never neglect being faithful to their local, Bible-believing church. However, attending church does not mean you are serving. Many people sit in a pew and warm 18 inches of real estate: that is not serving. The writer of Hebrews begins the admonition above stating, *"provoke"* one another. Only servants provoke others to serve.

It has been wisely said this way: "There are three types of people in the church: those who know what's happening, those who make things happen, and those who wonder, 'What just happened?'" Which are you? Get busy!

CHAPTER EIGHT

SACRIFICE!

There has never been a greater sacrifice than Jesus Christ. He gave fully of Himself, allowing Himself to be sacrificed as a Lamb before the slaughter.

"Who, being in the form of God, thought it not robbery to be equal with God: But made Himself of no reputation, and took upon Him the form of a servant, and was made in the likeness of men: And being found in fashion as a man, He humbled Himself, and became obedient unto death, even the death of the cross."

- Philippians 2:6-8

Jesus sacrificed His office, His position, and His life for you and me. He is the greatest sacrifice. In Philippians 2, Paul began this commendation by making the statement, *"Let this mind be in you, which was also in Christ Jesus [...]"* Paul spoke here of humility, but humility begins with sacrifice. Humility requires me to lay down that which I have.

The heart of a true Christ-follower is to be like Christ and to be like Christ, we must sacrifice ourselves.

While every one of us may be called to sacrifice different specific things, the areas of sacrifice are always the same.

The Sacrifice of Your Body

"I beseech you therefore, brethren, by the mercies of God, that ye present your bodies a living sacrifice, holy, acceptable unto God, which is your reasonable service."

- Romans 12:1

The first area every Christian is called to sacrifice is of their body. Paul is not speaking about that of taking our own life; rather he said we are to offer, *"a living sacrifice."* He continued by saying this sacrifice should be *"holy"* and *"acceptable unto God."* God expects His disciples to live holy lives.

This brings us full circle to the principle of sanctification, which we addressed in Chapter Six. Our lives should be sanctified, set-apart. Our head (what we think), our hands (what we do), our hearts (what we love), and our feet (where we go) are all to be set apart for Christ, sanctified for His purpose and will.

We are told that sacrificing ourselves unto Him is just our *"reasonable service."* It is reasonable that we would give to Him all we have, especially in light of the fact that He gave to us all He is.

The body you have been given is only a temporal shell to be used for the honor of Jesus Christ. In fact, it is only borrowed and put in your care to steward. It ultimately belongs to your Savior and houses the Holy Spirit.

"What? Know ye not that your body is the temple of the Holy Ghost which is in you, which ye have of God, and ye are not your own? For ye are bought with a price: therefore glorify God in your body, and in your spirit, which are God's."

- I Corinthians 6:19-20

The moment you trusted Christ as your Savior, the Holy Spirit took up residence in you. Your body--how you dress it, how you feed it, how you treat it— is His and should all be used for His glory.

I have never met anyone who had their home burglarized, robbed, or vandalized that was not upset by this violation. The Holy Spirit is much the same. When you suck on your cigarette, drink your alcohol, or gorge on your meal, you are vandalizing what belongs to Him. When you mark yourself with tattoos or put on that provocative attire, you are defacing His residence. When you view the wicked and perverse, you are opening the windows of His home to that which He despises.

The Sacrifice of Your Mind

If you are saved, you have been bought with a price. Your body is no longer yours: it is His. You and I, however, can never sacrifice our bodies unless we first learn to give our mind (our heart) to Him. The Bible often speaks of the heart and the mind interchangeably. This is because they both describe the inner part of man. In Proverbs we read, *"For as he thinketh in his heart, so is he [...]"* Our hearts are only surrendered to Him when our thoughts are given to Him.

"And be not conformed to this world: but be ye transformed by the renewing of your mind, that ye may prove what is that good, and acceptable, and perfect, will of God."

- Romans 12:2

We saw it previously in Philippians 2, when Paul said, *"Let this mind be in you [...]"* Our minds must be given to the things of God. Quite frankly, the reason so many Christians struggle to accept the comments about the sacrificing of our bodies is because our thoughts and our reasoning have not been transformed. We too often think with the carnal, selfish mind.

The renewing of the mind can only happen as we allow God's Word to penetrate our hearts, change the inner man, and transform our thoughts. The greatest battles you will face are not on the exterior, but rather they are the battles you face on the inside.

"For though we walk in the flesh, we do not war after the flesh: (For the weapons of our warfare are not carnal, but mighty through God to the pulling down of strong holds;) Casting down imaginations, and every high thing that exalteth itself against the knowledge of God, and bringing into captivity every thought to the obedience of Christ [...]"

- II Corinthians 10:3-5

The disciple of Christ is one who gives his mind (his thoughts) sacrificially to the obedience of Christ. How do we know when our thoughts are obediently sacrificed? Paul gives us a good checklist:

"Finally, brethren, whatsoever things are true, whatsoever things are honest, whatsoever things are just, whatsoever things are pure, whatsoever things are lovely, whatsoever things are of good report; if there be any virtue, and if there be any praise, think on these things."

- Philippians 4:8

The Sacrifice of Your Desires

"What do you want to be when you grow up?" A simple question that we ask our children. One that causes a young person to examine all their experiences, though few, and all of their ambitions to dream of a profession that they'd love to do with the rest of their life.

I'll ask you the same question with a twist, "What do you want to be now that you're grown up?" Not as a career, but in character. What if we asked, "If you could have anything, what would it be?" Deep down Christian, what do you desire?

The desires of our heart include possessions, ambitions, and even relationships.

*"Wherefore seeing we also are compassed about with so great a cloud of witnesses, let us lay aside **every weight,** and the sin which doth so easily beset us, and let us run with patience the race that is set before us, Looking unto Jesus the author and finisher of our faith [...]"*

- Hebrews 12:1-2a

Christians are exhorted to lay aside every weight that keeps us from running our race. The weights referred to in this passage seem to imply not only sinful things necessarily, but any of the things that weigh us down.

For many Christians, what keeps them from doing what God wants them to do is the influence of people around them. Sometimes it is a friend, sometimes it is a co-worker, or sometimes (sadly) it is even a family member.

It is always wise to seek biblical counsel, but sometimes it is necessary to break fellowship with those who keep us from doing what God wills for us. The disciples in Matthew 4 left even their own father to follow Christ. The company of wrong crowds, a boyfriend or girlfriend, or other relationships, has far too often derailed the life of a servant.

Another weight that often keeps people out of the race is the area of ambition. I found myself in a battle with God for two years when He called me to preach. At the time I had been in the Navy for seven years, I was on a fast track to advancement, and I desired nothing more than to serve until retirement. God had other plans for me and after nine years in the Navy, I laid my weight down and I have never regretted it.

Still others find themselves grappling with God over that thing they have always wanted or may have already obtained. It keeps them from spending the time with God that they know they should. It is the focus of their affection, time, or investment. For some, it may be money. Every time the offering plate is passed, they cringe. For others, it is that boat, retirement package, or TV show. In and of themselves, these things are not necessarily sinful, but left unchecked, they can easily weigh us down and keep us from following God like we should.

Is there something that God is calling for you to sacrifice? The Christian life is a life of sacrifice. Jesus gave His all for you: He deserves your all for Him. Sacrifice!

"And every one that hath forsaken houses, or brethren, or sisters, or father, or mother, or wife, or children, or lands, for My name's sake, shall receive an hundredfold, and shall inherit everlasting life."

- Matthew 19:29

Final Thoughts

"And He said to them all, If any man will come after Me, let him deny himself, and take up his cross daily, and follow Me."

- Luke 9:23

Our society is in desperate need of Christians who will shine their light. We live in a generation suffering a degeneration of morals. Our compass is off. This decline in morals has not only affected society as a whole, but also has affected "Christians."

The Christian life is one in which we "follow Christ." A Christian is not one influenced by the world and is not one that mimics the behaviors and patterns of our society. It is not one that strives for selfish ambitions. A Christian is a Christ-follower and a Christ-like life strives for His glory.

It is my prayer that a new generation of true Christians will rise up, that experienced Christians will turn again to Him, and that unbelievers would see in us a light shining brightly to glorify the Father!

SHINE!

www.ingramcontent.com/pod-product-compliance
Lightning Source LLC
Chambersburg PA
CBHW072017290426
44109CB00018B/2262